Make IT Now —
Bake IT Later!

Make IT Now -
Bake IT Later!

Make Each Dish in The Morning
Then Gently Set IT Aside.
Bring IT Forth That Evening
And Serve Your Guests with Pride.

Three Books In One!

by Barbara Goodfellow

A Fireside Book Published by
Simon and Schuster

A Fireside Book
Published by Simon and Schuster
A Gulf + Western Company
Rockefeller Center, 630 Fifth Avenue
New York, New York 10020

ISBN 0-671-22647-9
Library of Congress Catalog Card Number 65-24035
Manufactured in the United States of America

1 2 3 4 5 6 7 8 9 10

Make IT Now —
Bake IT Later!

Shrimp and Cheese Casserole

An all time favorite! Serve this at
your next party, and you will agree.

6 slices white bread
1 pound prepared shrimp (ready to eat)
1/2 pound Old English cheese (usually comes
    sliced)
1/4 cup margarine or butter, melted
1/2 teasp. dry mustard – salt to taste
3 whole eggs, beaten
1 pint milk

Break bread in pieces about size of a
    quarter.
Break cheese into bite size pieces.
Arrange shrimp, bread, and cheese in
    several layers in greased casserole.
Pour margarine or butter over this mixture.
Beat eggs. Add mustard and salt to eggs.
    Then add the milk. Mix together
    and pour this over ingredients in
    casserole.
Let stand a minimum of 3 hours,
    preferably overnight in refrigerator,
    covered.

Bake one hour in 350° oven, covered.

Naturally if you slightly increase the
    amount of shrimp, you improve
    the dish – but it is fine "as is."
    When doubling the recipe, use
    3 pounds of shrimp. Serves 4

1

Easy Chicken Casserole

"Easy" is right!

1 cup uncooked rice
1 can mushroom soup
1 pkg. dehydrated onion soup
1 ½ soup cans of milk
1 large fryer, cut in serving pieces
    salt and pepper

Mix together the rice, soups, and milk. Place in a large casserole. (I use a 3 qt. size)

Put the chicken on top, skin side down and add salt and pepper to taste.

Make this 3 hours ahead of time. Place it in a 250° oven, uncovered, for 3 hours. Turn the chicken over once. That's all!

Serves 4

2

Greco

Inexpensive and different!

1 yellow onion, chopped
1 green pepper, chopped
1 or 2 small cans mushrooms, drained
2 cups shell macaroni
3 cans Tomato sauce
1 can cream style corn
   sharp cheese
1 pound ground round or chuck

Fry onion and green pepper in
   small amount of oil until glossy.
Brown ground meat in above. Keep
   moving to prevent burning.
Add mushrooms and remove from heat.
Boil macaroni until tender. Drain
   and add to above.
Add Tomato sauce and corn and
   mix all well.
Place in greased casserole and
   refrigerate.

When ready to bake, grate lots of
   sharp cheese on top and place
   in 300° oven for 1 hour.

Serves 6

3

Crab and Shrimp

Fit for an embassy buffet!

1 1/2 pounds crabmeat
1/2 pound small shrimp
1/2 green pepper, chopped
1/3 cup parsley, chopped
2 cups cooked rice
1 1/2 cups real mayonnaise
2 packages frozen peas, thawed but not cooked
salt and pepper to taste

Toss lightly. Place in greased casserole. Refrigerate, covered.

Bake 1 hour at 350°, covered.

Serves 6

Teen Mix

A special favorite of Teenagers - who consume this in quantity!

4 slices bacon
1/2 large yellow onion, chopped
1 lb. very lean ground beef
1 large can baked beans (1 lb. 12 oz.) undrained
1 large can solid pack Tomatoes, undrained
1 Teasp. Worcestershire Sauce
1/8 Teasp. garlic salt
1 heaping Teasp. granulated sugar
  salt & pepper To Taste

Cut bacon in strips and cook Them with the onion in a large heavy kettle like a Dutch oven. Do not brown bacon until crisp - it should be barely cooked.

Add ground beef and brown slightly. Drain off all excess fat.

Add remaining ingredients and stir gently.

Cover kettle and simmer 1 1/4 hours. Stir occasionally To prevent sticking.

This may be made ahead and reheated for 4 To 6 hungry Teenagers.

Note: If you prefer it less juicy, do not use all The liquid with canned Tomatoes.

Cambridge Chicken with Ham

Another "day ahead" one!

1 large fryer, cut in pieces
  flour, mixed with a little salt and pepper
1/4 lb. butter or margarine
1/4 cup chopped green onions
1 4-oz. can mushrooms, drained
1 slice ham, diced
1 clove garlic, minced
  pinch of Thyme
  salt and pepper to taste
1 cup red wine

Shake chicken piece by piece in a paper bag containing the flour.

Brown chicken in butter and place in casserole.

Mix together all the remaining ingredients and pour over chicken. Spoon the juice over the chicken so it is well saturated.

Bake, covered, in a 350° oven for 1 hour.

Remove and cool for a short time before placing in the refrigerator overnight.

The next day, when ready to bake, again spoon the liquid over the chicken and place, covered, in a 300° oven for 1 hour.

Serves 4

6

Family Dinner for Four

Meat, potatoes, and vegetables, all in one!

1 lb lean ground chuck
   salt and pepper to taste
4 medium sized potatoes
   sliced onions, according to your taste
1/2 teasp. Worcestershire sauce
1 large can solid pack tomatoes

Brown the meat with the onions and add
   salt and pepper.
Peel potatoes and slice them into a 2 qt.
   casserole.
Place meat and onions on top of potatoes.
Add Worcestershire to the tomatoes –
   do not drain them – and pour
   this over all.
Refrigerate.

When ready to bake, place in 350° oven,
   covered, for 1 1/2 hours or until potatoes
   are done.
Note: If you want to be fancier, you
   may add 2 cups diced celery and
   1/2 cup diced green pepper. Arrange
   in layers with the potatoes.

Serves 4

Stroganoff Bake

No last minute mixing in this Stroganoff.

6 slices bacon, cooked
2 pounds veal cut in large bite size pieces
2 large yellow onions, chopped
1/2 pound fresh mushrooms
1 pint commercial sour cream
1 cup white cooking wine
1 cup raw white rice

Set cooked bacon aside and brown veal
    in bacon grease. Remove from pan.
Brown onions in pan.
Slice mushrooms.
Combine veal, onions, and mushrooms,
    and add the sour cream which you
    have mixed with wine.
Cover and cook slowly on top stove for
    2 hours. Stir occasionally.
Boil rice, drain, and combine with
    above mixture in layers. Refrigerate.
When ready to bake, crumble cooked
    bacon on top and bake, uncovered,
    at 300° for one hour or until
    piping hot.
Serves 6

8

Savory Sausage Casserole

Inexpensive and Tasty!

1 lb. bulk pork sausage (a good brand not too salty!)
1 cup uncooked rice
2 pkgs. (2 oz. each) dehydrated chicken
  noodle soup
1/4 cup finely chopped onion
1 cup sliced celery
2 1/2 cups water
1 Tblsp. soy sauce
1/2 cup toasted halved or slivered blanched
  almonds

Break apart the sausage and brown it in
  an ungreased skillet, pouring off any
  excess fat as it accumulates. Remove
  from the burner.

Mix together the sausage, rice, soup,
  onion, and celery and place in a
  2 qt. casserole.

Refrigerate.

When ready to bake, mix soy sauce with
  water and add this, with the almonds,
  to the casserole. Mix all gently.

Cover and bake at 350 for 1 hour.

Serves 6

Long Beach Seafood

A certain hit - and so easy!

2 cans frozen shrimp soup
2 Tblsp. sherry
2 small cans button mushrooms, drained
1 pkg. slivered almonds (about 2½ oz.)
½ lb. fresh crabmeat
½ lb. fresh shrimp, small size
   Sliced American cheese
   paprika

Melt soup according to directions on the
   can. Melt only-don't add milk or water!
Place melted soup in 2 qt. casserole and
   stir in sherry, mushrooms, and almonds.
Fold in seafood gently and cover with one
   layer of sliced cheese (not just one slice!)
Sprinkle paprika on top.

Refrigerate.

When ready to bake, place in 300° oven,
   uncovered, for one hour. Serve over
   hot fluffy rice.
Note: Lobster and prawns may be used as
   substitutes. Frozen seafood may be
   used if you cannot obtain fresh.
Serves 6

Spanish Bean Pot

A delicious new version of an old favorite.

2 large (# 2½) cans red kidney beans
3 slices bacon
1 yellow onion
½ cup juice from can of peach halves
2 Tblsp. cider vinegar
¼ cup strong coffee

Drain beans, saving liquid.
Fry bacon and cut in small pieces.
Slice onion and fry in bacon grease.

Combine the above.

Then combine the following:
  1 clove garlic, grated
  1 pinch thyme
  1 pinch rosemary
  1 Tsp. salt
  1 bay leaf, broken
  2 Tsp. dry mustard
  ¼ Tsp. ground cloves
  ¼ Tsp. cayenne

Combine this second mixture
  with the first.   (cont'd)

Spanish Bean Pot (cont'd)

Place in greased casserole and refrigerate.

When ready to bake, place in very
slow oven 1 to 1½ hours.
Put 4 slices bacon on top the last
½ hour.
If it becomes too dry, add some
bean liquor.
Just before serving, add 1 jigger
brandy and stir casserole up
from the bottom to mix.

This can be made a day ahead,
baked when ready.

Peaches can be served as a side
dish with the beans.

If you double the recipe, do not
fully double the fruit juice
unless you want beans to
be very juicy!

Serves 6

Chinese Casserole

The unusual flavor and crunchiness of this dish give it a personality all its own.

2 cans solid pack Tuna
1 can mushroom soup
1/4 cup water
1 Tblsp. soy sauce
1 cup whole cashew nuts
1 4-oz. can button mushrooms, drained
2 cups canned Chinese Chow Mein noodles
1/4 cup minced onion or chopped green onion Tops
1 cup chopped celery

Drain Tuna and break it into bite size
  chunks.
Mix Together The mushroom soup, water,
  and soy sauce.
Combine Tuna, mushroom soup mixture,
  and all remaining ingredients except 1
  cup of The noodles.
Mix gently and place in casserole.
Refrigerate.

When ready To bake, sprinkle remaining
  cup of noodles on Top and bake at
  375°, uncovered, for 40 minutes.

Serves 6

London Chicken

So simple - and so delicious!

24 pieces of chicken (breasts, legs, and second joints)
butter (enough to brown chicken)
3/4 lb sliced mushrooms (can use canned, drained)
2 cans cream of chicken soup
1 can mushroom soup
sherry or white wine to taste. (about 1/4 cup)

Brown the chicken in butter. Then brown mushrooms if using fresh ones.

Place chicken in a large casserole.

Mix the soups (undiluted) and pour over chicken.

Place mushrooms on top.

Refrigerate.

When ready to bake, add wine, cover the casserole, and bake at 350° for 1 1/2 hours.

Serves 12

14

Sausage Casserole for Six

Your family will love this, and for company
serve it with dry red wine, green salad,
and French bread!

1 pound pork sausage (not highly seasoned)
½ green pepper, chopped
1 large can Tomatoes, mashed but not drained
6 bay leaves
  dash paprika
½ Tsp. Worcestershire sauce
1 pkg. fine noodles cooked in salted water
  Parmesan cheese

Crumble sausage and cook slowly until brown.
  Remove from pan and drain.
Sauté green pepper in 2 Tblsp. oil or sausage
  fat until glossy
Add all other ingredients to green pepper
  and simmer for 5 minutes, stirring
  occasionally.
Put all in greased casserole. Add salt
  and pepper if necessary.
Shake Parmesan cheese generously over top.
Refrigerate.

Bake uncovered 45 minutes at 350°
  until cheese is melted.
Serve with more Parmesan cheese.

Crab in Cups

Make a day ahead!

4 Tblsp butter, melted
4 Tblsp flour
1 Tsp wet mustard
1 Tsp salt
1 Tsp Worcestershire
Dash cayenne

1 cup canned Tomatoes, drained
1 cup mellow grated cheese
2 eggs, slightly beaten
1 1/2 cups milk
2 cups crabmeat in chunks

Blend flour into melted butter. Add next seven
   ingredients. Cook slowly, stirring often,
   about 5 minutes or until cheese melts.
Heat milk
Add seasoned ingredients to milk.
Add crab.
Let thicken in Top of double boiler. Stir
   occasionally. Refrigerate.

Reheat, uncovered, and serve in Toast cups -
   with a little parsley and paprika on Top.

Toast Cups

Rub muffin Tins with margarine.
Decrust sliced bread. Push into cups.
Bake at 275° until golden brown.
Reheat on cookie sheet.

Serves 6

Wild Rice Party Casserole

A special favorite!

2 cups boiling water
2/3 cup uncooked wild rice
1 can chicken rice soup
1 small can mushrooms, undrained
1/2 cup water
1 Teasp. salt
1 bay leaf
1/4 Teasp. each of celery salt, garlic salt,
   pepper, onion salt, and paprika.
3 Tblsp. chopped onion
3 Tblsp. salad oil
3/4 lb. lean ground beef

Pour boiling water over rice. Let stand,
   covered, 15 minutes. Drain.
Place rice in a 2 qt. casserole.
Add soup, mushrooms with liquid, water,
   and seasonings. Mix gently and let
   stand a few minutes.
Sauté onions in oil until glossy. Remove
   and add to casserole.
Add meat to frying pan and fry, stirring
   gently until brown and crumbly.
Add to rice and refrigerate.
When ready, bake 2 hours at 325°, covered.
Serves 4   17

Baked Salad

Make it, bake it, and serve it hot for
buffet supper - or make it, don't bake
it and serve it on lettuce for luncheon -
or make it, bake it, serve it, and place
remainder in refrigerator for a delectable
leftover. No matter what, it's extra-special

1 cup chopped green pepper
½ cup chopped yellow onion
2 cups chopped celery
2 cups real mayonnaise
2 cans crabmeat (approximately 2 cups)
2 cans shrimp, drained   " " "
1 can lobster
1 can chunk or solid pack Tuna
1 Tsp. Worcestershire
1 Tsp. salt
  pepper to taste
  dash of Tabasco
  potato chips for Topping

Mix all gently except chips. Refrigerate.
Crush chips and put on top.
Bake at 350° for ½ hour or until
  hot Through.

Can be made a day ahead as marinating
  improves flavor!
Serves 6. Double for a luncheon for
  12 or dinner for 10.

18

Egg-Asparagus-Mushroom Casserole

A wonderful Friday luncheon dish!

2 Tblsp. butter
3 Tblsp. flour
½ Teasp. prepared brown mustard
1 can mushroom soup
1 large can green asparagus Tips
4 hard cooked eggs, sliced
½ cup rice flakes, crushed before measuring
¼ cup grated American cheese

Melt butter, add flour, and blend well.

Combine mustard with soup and add to
    flour-mixture. Cook slowly, stirring
    constantly, until Thick.
In a buttered casserole arrange a layer
    of asparagus, Then a layer of eggs
    and some of The sauce. Repeat
    layers until all is used.
Refrigerate - or just set aside.
When ready To bake, combine rice flakes
    and grated cheese and sprinkle over
    The Top.
Place in a 350° oven, uncovered, and
    bake until hot Through - about
    35 minutes.

Serves 5   19

Sausage and Veal

A family favorite!

1/2 lb. pork sausage
2 lbs. boneless veal cut in 2 inch cubes
1 cup all purpose flour
1 medium yellow onion, chopped
1 Teasp. paprika
1/2 Teasp. basil
1/4 Teasp. Thyme
3/4 cup dry white wine

Brown sausage lightly. Remove from pan.

Dredge veal with flour. Brown in sausage drippings. Pour off all excess grease.

Add sausage, onion, paprika, basil, and Thyme and place in 2 QT. casserole.

Pour wine over casserole, cover, and refrigerate.

When ready, bake, covered, at 350° for 1 1/2 hours.

Serve over hot noodles using The delicious juice from casserole as gravy.

20   Serves 5

Party Chicken

A new combination but still so easy!

8 good sized chicken breasts
  Ask your meat man To skin and
  bone Them.
8 slices bacon
1 pkg. chipped beef - about 4 oz.
1 can undiluted mushroom soup
½ pint commercial sour cream

Wrap each chicken breast with a
  piece of bacon.
Cover bottom of flat greased baking
  dish (about 8" x 12" x 2") with
  chipped beef.
Arrange chicken breasts on chipped
  beef.
Mix soup and sour cream and pour over
  all. Refrigerate.
When ready, bake at 275° for 3 hours,
  uncovered.

Serves 8 ⌐

21

Rice and Shrimp Casserole

An entirely differently flavored shrimp dish, and _so_ good!

2 pounds shrimp - or 1 pound already cooked and prepared
1/3 cup onion, chopped and browned in
2 Tblsp. margarine
1 or 2 cloves minced garlic
1 cup raw white rice
1 large can Tomatoes, not drained
2 cups chicken bouillon
1 bay leaf broken in pieces
3 Tblsp. chopped parsley
1/2 Tsp. ground cloves
1/2 Tsp Marjoram
1 Tsp. chili powder
dash cayenne
1 Tsp salt
1/8 Tsp pepper

Combine onion, garlic, rice, bay leaf, parsley, cloves, marjoram, chili powder, cayenne, salt, and pepper in casserole. Mix gently.
Combine Tomatoes and bouillon.

Just before baking, add wet ingredients to dry, add shrimp, and mix.
Bake 1 1/2 hours at 350°, covered.

Serves 6

22

Sausages and Apples

Even your children will love This!

2 large or 3 small very Tart apples
   brown sugar
1 cup long grain raw rice
2 cups cold water - brought To a boil.
   salt
1 pkg. best quality links sausages
      (not The precooked ones)
¼ cup ketchup - no more

Core and slice apples but do not peel.
Cover bottom of 2 qt. casserole with apples.
Cover apples with brown sugar.
In the meanTime be boiling The rice
      in The salted water. Rice will be
      done when water is absorbed.
Cover apples and sugar with rice.
Pour more boiling water over
      sausages and let stand 3 minutes.
      Drain. (This absorbs grease.)
Arrange sausages close Together on rice.
Frost with ketchup and refrigerate.
When ready, bake at 350° for 45
      minutes To 1 hour. Uncover last
      15 minutes.   Serves 4 -

23

Clam in Shells

Make the night before and store in refrigerator. Makes 5 shells.

5 Tblsp. flour
4 Tblsp. butter
2 cans minced clams, drained - save juice
4 egg yolks beaten until light
2 Tblsp. chopped fresh parsley
2 Teasp. chopped onion
    salt and cayenne
    buttered crumbs

Make thick white sauce with flour, butter, and juice of clams.

When thoroughly blended (use wire whip) add egg yolks slowly, by Teaspoon at first, so they won't string.

Add parsley, onion, pinch of salt and cayenne.

Mix in drained clams.

Place in shells and sprinkle with crumbs which you have toasted in a little butter. Refrigerate.

Put shells in pan with warm water to cover bottom of shells and brown in 375° oven 20-25 minutes.

24

Meat Balls!

1½ lbs ground round steak
1 pkg. dry onion soup mix
1 cup water
2 8-oz. cans Tomato sauce
½ Teasp. garlic salt
½ Teasp. Thyme
½ Teasp. pepper
½ Teasp. Oregano
1 Teasp. dehydrated parsley flakes

Set meat aside while you cook on Top
  the stove for a very short Time
  The soup mix and water.
While This is simmering, open Tomato
  sauce and pour about 2 Tblsp. of
  it into a cup. To This add The
  garlic salt, Thyme, pepper, oregano,
  and parsley flakes. Stir it all
  well and Then mix it Thoroughly
  with The ground beef.
Add remaining Tomato sauce To The
  simmering onion soup. Stir
  carefully.
Make beef mixture into meatballs The size
  of a small egg and place in a
  2 qt. casserole. Over This pour
  The sauce. Refrigerate, covered.
Bake at 350, covered, for one hour.
Serve over spiced, or wild, or plain rice.
Makes about 20 meatballs.

Crispy Chicken

Simple and Tasty for company or family.

1 chicken, cut in pieces
1/4 lb. butter, melted
1 pkg. Pepperidge Farm Stuffing
   (You really will need only 1/2 pkg. for
   1 chicken.)
Salt and pepper to taste.

First roll out the stuffing with a
   rolling pin to make crumbs.

Then dip the chicken, piece by piece,
   in the butter and roll it until
   covered in the stuffing crumbs.

Place in a shallow baking pan or on
   a cookie sheet and sprinkle with
   salt and pepper lightly. Refrigerate.

When ready to bake, place in a 350°
   oven for 1 1/4 hours.

(For company use breasts, thighs, and
   legs.)

Serves 4

26

Lobster Newburg

You can keep the makings for this
on your pantry shelf! Serves 6.

1 can lobster
1 can crabmeat
1 can shrimp
4 Tblsp. butter
1/2 Teasp. paprika
1/4 Teasp. nutmeg
2 cans Cream of Mushroom soup
1 can (3 oz.) sliced mushrooms - save juice
1 can evaporated milk - regular size
1/4 Teasp. salt
1/4 cup sherry

Melt butter in large skillet.
Wash seafood and sauté it in the
   butter for about 5 minutes.
Sprinkle on the paprika and nutmeg
   and stir a bit.
Mix together the soup, mushrooms (in-
   cluding liquid from can) and milk.
   Pour this over seafood.
Add salt and mix all gently. Simmer
   for 10 minutes. Stir occasionally to
   prevent sticking.
Refrigerate in large bowl.
Reheat in top of double boiler, uncovered.
When piping hot, add sherry and serve
   over rice, in patty shells, or on toast.

27

Lamb Shanks Deluxe

And so fragrant while baking!

4 meaty lamb shanks
1/2 lemon
1/4 Tsp. garlic powder - or more
1 cup all-purpose flour
2 Tsp. salt
1/2 Tsp. pepper
1/2 cup salad oil
1 can (10 1/2 oz.) condensed beef con-
        sommé, undiluted
1 cup water
1/2 cup dry vermouth
1 medium yellow onion, chopped
4 carrots, peeled and sliced in chunks
4 stalks celery, sliced in chunks

Rub lamb with lemon and sprinkle
    with garlic powder. Let stand 10
    minutes.
Combine flour, salt, and pepper in a
    paper bag. Shake shanks one at a
    time in bag to coat with flour.
    Save flour.
Brown shanks in hot oil in large
    heavy skillet. Remove meat from
    pan.
        (cont'd)
        28

Lamb Shanks Deluxe (cont'd)

A 4 Tblsp. of the seasoned flour to
pan drippings and, using a wire
whip, stir and brown the flour.

Add consommé, water, and vermouth
and stir and cook until slightly
thickened. Add onion.

Place shanks in large baking dish
and pour over them the consommé
mixture. Shanks should be in
one layer only. Refrigerate.

When ready to bake, place in 350°
oven, uncovered, for 1½ hours.

Turn shanks, add carrots and celery,
and continue to bake one
more hour.

Gravy delicious over mashed potatoes.

Serves 4

29

Chicken Tamale

A real "company" dish!

3 Tamales cut into bite size pieces
    (or use 2 jars)
1 cup canned Tomato pulp (drain solid
    pack Tomatoes well)
1 small can whole kernel corn
1 cup chopped or sliced olives (ripe)
½ cup chili sauce
1 Tblsp. olive or salad oil.
1 Tblsp. Worcestershire sauce
1 cup grated cheese
2 cups cooked chicken cut into
    good sized chunks (The equiva-
    lent of 1 large stew hen.)

Mix The above except cheese and
    store in casserole in refrigerator.

When ready To bake, cover with
    grated cheese and bake 1
    hour at 350°.

Serves 6 To 8

Picnic Barbecue

When your relatives and all the children
are coming, This is for you!

1 can corned beef, chopped
4 medium yellow onions, chopped
2 stalks celery, chopped
1 cup drained canned Tomatoes
1 1/2 cups water
1 Tblsp. chili powder
1 Tblsp. vinegar
3 Tblsp Worcestershire sauce
1/4 cup chili sauce

Saute onions and celery in a little oil
until glossy.
Add all other ingredients and simmer
very slowly, uncovered, 1 To 1 1/2
hours. Add a little more water
if it becomes Too dry.

Reheat and serve in warm hamburger
buns.

Serves 6

Curried Shrimp
Quick and Tasty!

1 can Cream of Mushroom soup
1 4-oz. can mushrooms, undrained
½ Tsp. Worcestershire
¼ Tsp. dry mustard
½ Tsp. curry powder
⅛ Tsp. pepper
¾ lb. fresh cooked shrimp – or 2 or 3
      cans, drained and washed.
½ cup slivered almonds, Toasted lightly
      in a little butter

Mix soup, undrained mushrooms, and
      seasonings.
Add shrimp. Refrigerate.

To serve, heat in Top of double boiler
      until piping hot. Add nuts.
Serve over hot fluffy white rice – with
      a fruit salad.
Have plenty of chutney on hand when
      serving curry!

Serves 4 —

Captain's Casserole

A delicious double duty dish!

2 fryers, cut in pieces (minus giblets)
  salt and pepper
½ lb. butter
1 large yellow onion, thinly sliced
1 green pepper, thinly sliced
2 cans solid pack tomatoes, 1 lb. 12 oz. each
½ teasp. garlic powder
1 teasp. salt
½ teasp. pepper
1 tblsp. chopped parsley
½ teasp. powdered thyme
½ teas p. oregano
1 heaping tblsp. curry powder

Sprinkle chicken with salt and pepper and fry
  quickly in butter until golden brown. Remove.
Into the butter now put onions and peppers and fry
  slowly until glossy.
Mix remaining ingredients into undrained tomatoes,
  but chop up tomatoes a bit. Add this to
  onions and peppers and cook, slowly, 5 minutes.
In a 3 qt casserole arrange chicken, pour the
  sauce over it and refrigerate till baking time.
Bake, covered, for 1¼ hours at 350°. Serve with
  wild rice or brown rice to 8. Be sure to serve
  with this plenty of mustard pickle!

I find I have 2 qts. sauce remaining. Freeze it. Then
  thaw, add 1 can cream of shrimp soup, 5 lbs
  prepared shrimp. When all is piping hot, serve
  with fluffy rice to 10 or 12 more guests.

33

Crab and Shrimp with Almonds

With a crispy Touch!

1 generous cup crab
1 generous cup shrimp
2 cans undiluted mushroom soup
1 cup finely chopped celery
1/4 cup minced green onions
1 can (3 oz.) Chinese fried noodles
1 pkg. (2 oz.) slivered almonds

Combine first five ingredients
and place in greased 2 qt.
casserole. Refrigerate.

When ready to bake, fold in noodles
Top with almonds, and bake at
375° uncovered for 25 minutes
or until piping hot.

(I usually lightly brown The
almonds first in a little butter-
slowly as They burn easily.)

Serves 6

Pizza Pie

For the Teenage cooks!

1 lb lean ground beef
½ Tsp. salt
¼ Tsp. pepper
1 cup well drained canned Tomatoes
    Use a good brand which contains
    more Tomatoes Than juice.
½ cup freshly shredded sharp cheese.
2 Tblsp. finely chopped onion
2 Tblsp. chopped parsley (cut with scissors)
¼ Teasp. dried basil
¼ Teasp. oregano

Mix beef with salt and pepper and pat
    out in a 9" pie plate.
Spread Tomatoes over meat and sprinkle
    with remaining ingredients.
Refrigerate.
When ready, bake in a 375° oven
    for a good 20 minutes.
Cut in wedges To serve 4.

Clam and Corn Souffle

A real Taste Teaser. No one will guess what is in it.

1¼ cup crumbled soda crackers.
1 cup milk
2 eggs, beaten
1 can minced clams, undrained
1 cup frozen corn
    (½ pkg. - Thawed but not cooked)
3 Tblsp. melted butter
2 Tblsp. minced onion
¼ Teasp. salt
½ Teasp. Worcestershire
½ cup shredded sharp cheese.

Soak crackers until soggy in milk and
    eggs - about half an hour.
Then add all but the cheese.
Mix gently and refrigerate in a
    1½ Qt. casserole.
When ready to bake, place casserole,
    uncovered, in 300° oven for
    50 minutes.
Sprinkle cheese on top and allow it
    to bake just long enough to
    melt cheese - about 10 minutes.
Good with Molded Salad on page 69.

Serves 4

36

Lobster Sturdevant

Serve this on a hot, sultry night in shells or ramekins with a green salad and corn pudding. It is just right!

Cheese glass of real mayonnaise
A little less than a cheese glass of catsup.
½ jigger of chives (I cut them in bits with scissors.)
½ cup lemon juice
Lots of paprika (about 1 Tsp.)
1 jigger brandy
1 pound prepared lobster or crab-meat

Mix and store in refrigerator.
Serve cold.

These are certainly unusual directions, but it is the way it was told to me, and I must say I would have a hard time measuring ½ oz. of chives!

Serves 4

Veal Vermouth

Somewhat like a Veal Stew - very tasty!

2 lbs veal cutlets, cut into serving size
    pieces - or a little smaller
    Salt and pepper to taste
    Parmesan Cheese (finely grated)
    Butter or margarine
2 large onions, chopped
4 or 5 carrots, sliced - not too thin
1 cup mushrooms, sliced (about 1/2 lb.)
3 chicken bouillon cubes
1 1/2 cup boiling water
1/2 cup Vermouth or any white wine

Sprinkle cutlets with salt, pepper, and
    cheese.
Brown them in butter in a heavy skillet.
Place them in a 3 qt. casserole.
Now sauté the onions, carrots, and
    mushrooms in the skillet. Add more
    butter if necessary.
Meanwhile dissolve bouillon cubes in water
    and add wine. Pour over the semi-
    cooked vegetables. Then pour all over
    veal. Refrigerate casserole.
Bake, covered, at 325° for one hour.
Serves 5.
Juice is excellent over noodles, rice, or
    mashed potatoes.

Friday Favorite

Quick, easy, and delicious!

2 lbs skinned Haddock fillets
  Dijon mustard
  Salt and pepper to taste
½ cup cracker crumbs (the square
    small white type) seasoned
    with ¼ Teasp. salt, ¼ Teasp.
    pepper, ⅛ Teasp. oregano or
    Thyme.
  Parsley
  Lemon

Spread fillets lightly with mustard
  on both sides.
Sprinkle with salt and pepper.
Roll in cracker crumbs.
Refrigerate.

Heat oven to 500°.
Grease flat baking dish and heat thoroughly.
Lay fish in dish and bake at 500° for 10
  minutes.
Decorate with sprigs of parsley and serve
  with lemon wedges.

                Serves 4 or 5.

Not Navy Beans
The best you ever ate!

1 pkg. dry red kidney beans - 1 lb. size
1 clove garlic, minced
1 ham end with plenty of meat on the
    bone - at least 3 lbs.
1 bottle chili sauce
½ bottle ketchup

Soak the beans overnight.
The next morning drain the beans, place
    them in a kettle, and cover them with
    water.
Add the garlic.
Add ham end, skin and all.
Simmer beans until they begin to soften -
    about 3 hours. Add water if necessary
    during cooking to keep beans covered. Don't
    worry if beans burst!
Remove ham end. Take off the skin. Remove
    meat from bone and cut in large bite size
    chunks. Return chunks to the beans.
    Simmer one hour more.
Drain beans except for about 1 cup bean liquor.
Add chili and ketchup to beans and mix gently.
Reheat slowly about 20 minutes until piping hot.
May be refrigerated and reheated - but keep it
    moist by adding more ketchup. Heat slowly!
Serves 6 to 8

40

Deviled Crab
This one can be prepared a day ahead, too!

1/4 cube butter
1 large onion, minced
2 stalks celery, chopped fine
1 1/2 pounds crabmeat, shredded
2 or 3 slices bread, toasted and crumbled fine
1 Tblsp. Worcestershire sauce
Dash cayenne
Salt and pepper
1/2 Tsp. dry mustard
mayonnaise

Fry onion and celery slowly in butter
  until glossy. Remove from flame.
Add crab
Mix together the Worcestershire, cayenne,
  salt, pepper, and mustard. Add to
  crab mixture.
Add enough mayonnaise to hold together.
Refrigerate in shells or small individual
  baking dishes.

When ready to bake, sprinkle with
  crumbs, dot with butter, and place
  in 400°-450° oven for 15 minutes.

Serves 6-8

41

Sophisticated Stew

A real "company" dish!

3 lbs lean round or chuck cut into large
    bite size pieces
  paper bag of flour seasoned with salt
    and pepper
6 strips of bacon
2 cloves of garlic, finely minced
1 oz. brandy, warmed
12 small whole fresh mushrooms
1 cup condensed beef bouillon
1½ cups dry red wine
12 small peeled white onions
12 small carrots, sliced
6 slightly bruised peppercorns
4 whole cloves
1 bay leaf, crumbled
2 Tblsp. chopped fresh parsley
¼ Teasp. dried marjoram
¼ Teasp. Thyme

Shake beef cubes in the flour, a few at
  a time until they are well covered.
In a large iron skillet fry the bacon
  until it begins to brown but is not crisp.
  Cut bacon into one inch pieces after
  cooking. Place in earthenware or heavy
  glass baking dish.

42   Cont'd

Sophisticated Stew (Cont'd)

Cook the garlic a little in the bacon-fat.

Then add the floured beef cubes and brown quickly on all sides, turning often.

Pour the brandy into the skillet, light it, and when flame dies out, remove the meat and garlic and put them in the casserole. (Garlic has probably disappeared by now.)

Put the mushrooms in skillet and brown lightly. Add them to casserole.

Put the bouillon and one cup of the red wine into skillet - bring to a boil and stir from the bottom to loosen the particles, using a wire whip. Pour the liquid into the casserole.

Add to the casserole the onions, carrots, peppercorns, cloves, bay leaf, parsley, marjoram, and thyme.

Now pour over the casserole your remaining 1/2 cup of red wine.

Cover the casserole tightly and bake at 300° for 2 hours. Cool, and place in refrigerator, covered.

When ready the next day, spoon some of the liquid up from the bottom over the meat and again place the casserole in a 300° oven, covered, and bake for 1 hour or until piping hot.

Serves 6

Quick Tamale

The family will love This

4 small cans chicken Tamale
2/3 can cream style corn
1/2 can pitted olives, drained (ripe)
1/3 cup grated cheese

Combine Tamale, corn, and olives.
Sprinkle cheese on Top.
Refrigerate

when ready To bake, place in
     350° oven, uncovered, for
     40 minutes.

Serves 4

Chicken Supper Dish
Really deluxe!

6 full breasts of chicken, cooked
1 large yellow onion, chopped
1 cup raw white rice
1 #2½ can solid pack Tomatoes, not drained
2 cloves garlic
2 small cans mushrooms, drained
½ green pepper, chopped

Simmer chicken until tender. Save the broth.
Remove chicken from bones in large chunks.
Fry onions and green pepper in a little oil
    until glossy.
Add raw rice and keep over low flame until
    golden brown.
Add Tomatoes, garlic, mushrooms and
    simmer about 20 minutes. Remove
    garlic.
Place chicken in greased casserole and
    spread rice mixture on top.
    Refrigerate after adding about
    one inch chicken broth to casserole.

Bake at 350° for 45 minutes. Add a little
    more broth if it seems dry.

Serves 6 generously

45

Crab and Spinach Casserole

Just right for luncheon or buffet supper.

2 pkgs. frozen chopped spinach
1 pound crabmeat
1 1/2 cups grated sharp cheese
1 cup finely chopped onions
1 can Tomato paste
1 cup commercial sour cream
   dash nutmeg
   salt and pepper

Thaw spinach.
Grate cheese.
Start with layer of spinach, Then
   onions, Then crab, Then cheese.
   Add nutmeg, salt, and pepper.
   Repeat once again. Refrigerate.
When ready To bake, put mixture
   of sour cream and tomato paste
   on Top.
Bake 45 minutes in 325° oven.

Serves 4.

Rice and Deviled Eggs with Tuna

Deluxe and Inexpensive!

1/4 cup green pepper, chopped
1/4 cup minced onion
2 Tblsp. butter
1/2 cup milk
1 can mushroom soup
2 cups cooked rice
1 cup flaked Tuna
3/4 cup grated cheddar cheese
1 cup bread crumbs, fried slowly in butter
6 deviled eggs

Cook green pepper and onions in butter until glossy
Combine soup and milk
To 3/4 of the soup mixture, add rice and Tuna.
Place in casserole.
Top with deviled eggs and refrigerate.
When ready to bake, pour over remaining
     soup mixture and sprinkle with buttered
     crumbs and cheese.
Bake at 350° 40 minutes.

Deviled Eggs

6 eggs, hard boiled
1/2 Tsp salt, 1/8 Tsp. pepper, 1 Tsp. wet mustard,
     1 Tsp horse-radish
1 Tsp minced parsley
1/4 cup mayonnaise

Cut eggs in half lengthwise. Mash yolk. Add
     other ingredients to yolks and mix well.
Fill egg whites

Serves 6

47

Easy Chicken with Onions

A delectable dish given to me by another Navy wife. You will use it happily often.

6 "meaty" chicken breasts
12 to 16 tiny whole white onions, peeled. If you are really in a rush, buy a bottled can of onions. It is an 8 1/2 oz. can and contains 10 to 12 onions.
1 can Cream of Mushroom soup.
1/8 cup sherry - or more
1/4 lb. cheddar cheese - freshly grated

Place chicken in baking dish.
Add onions.
Mix soup and sherry. Pour over chicken.
Grate cheese over top. Refrigerate.

When ready, place in 350° oven, covered, for 45 minutes. Uncover and continue baking for a good 30-45 minutes more.

(Somewhere along the line I usually add some salt and pepper.)

Serves 6

Crab Supreme

Make it a day ahead!

8 slices bread
2 cups crabmeat
1 yellow onion, chopped
1/2 cup mayonnaise
1 cup celery, chopped
1/2 cup green pepper, chopped

4 eggs, beaten
3 cups milk
1 cup canned mushroom soup
grated cheese
paprika

Cook celery slowly 10 minutes in a little water. Drain.
Dice half of bread into baking dish.
Mix crab, onion, mayonnaise, pepper, and celery and spread over bread.
Dice other slices of bread and place over crab mixture.
Mix eggs and milk together and pour over dish.
Cover and place in refrigerator overnight.

Bake for 15 minutes at 325° Then spoon soup over the top. Sprinkle top with cheese and paprika.
Bake one hour more or until golden brown.
Serves 8

Spaghetti Sauce

Everyone has her favorite, and this is mine.
Yes - I know you'll say I used everything
but the kitchen sink!

2 lbs lean ground beef
2 cloves garlic, minced
½ cup red wine
1 can mushrooms, undrained
1 pkg. dehydrated onion soup (1½ oz.)
2 teasp crushed basil leaves
½ teasp. salt
¼ teasp. pepper
   large pinch cinnamon
   large pinch allspice
3 Tblsp. chopped fresh parsley
1 large can solid pack tomatoes, undrained
1 can tomato paste (6 oz. size)
1 cup water - more or less depending on
   the consistency you want.

Brown meat and garlic in large iron frying
Add wine and simmer, stirring often, for 10
   minutes.
Add all remaining ingredients.
Cover pan almost completely (allowing space
   for steam to escape) and simmer 1 hour.
Toss with 12 oz. of steaming hot spaghetti
   and serve 8 hungry people.
This may be made ahead and refrigerated - or
frozen - or just made when desired.

Chicken Bake

My husband chuckled at This because To
him "Half and Half" is a brand of Tobacco.

1 good sized fryer, cut in pieces
2 eggs, beaten
About 2 cups of flour seasoned with salt
and pepper.
Margarine
1 cup "Half and Half" cream

Dip chicken pieces one by one in beaten
eggs and Then shake in paper bag
containing The flour. Place in refrigera-
Tor covered with wax paper.

When ready To bake, lay side by side
closely in baking dish or pan and dot
with margarine. Add 2 slices of
margarine To pan.

Place in 475° oven for 30 minutes. Tip
The pan a Time or Two To spread The
margarine on bottom of pan.

Pour Half and Half over chicken and bake
1 hour longer at 350°.

If chicken seems To be drying, you may
add more Half and Half.

Be sure To let Half and Half reach room
Temperature, or it will crack a baking dish.

Serves 4

Mushrooms and Rice

I could eat this every night!

2 2/3 cups precooked rice
6 Tblsp. salad oil
2 small cans mushrooms, drained
   green onions, chopped
2 cans beef consomme, undiluted
2 Tblsp soya sauce
1/2 Tsp. salt

Mix and bake, covered, at 350° until
   water is absorbed, no more than
   30-45 minutes. Do not stir.

To prepare in advance, place dry
   ingredients in casserole and
   add liquids just before baking.

Serves 6

California Barbecue

Try this at your next cookout!

5 cans macaroni with cheese sauce - 15 oz. size.
1 pkg. frozen chopped spinach
      Thawed and drained
½ lb. freshly grated sharp cheese
      Don't buy pregrated! Save some
      for Top when adding To casserole.
1 small bunch green onions, cut up finely
½ Tsp. oregano
1 can French fried onions.

Mix all Together except French fried onions.
      Remember To save some of the
      cheese and sprinkle it on Top.
Refrigerate.
Cover Top with French fried onions and
      bake, uncovered, in a 350° oven
      45 To 60 minutes until hot Through.

A 3 qt casserole is fine for This.

Serves 8

53

Tomato Side Dish

Your friends will ask, "How did you
   make This?"

2 large cans solid pack Tomatoes
8 whole cloves
8 whole peppercorns
1 bay leaf (at least 1 inch long)
   salt
1/2 yellow onion, chopped
3/4 cup brown sugar
3 or 4 slices white bread pulled into
   dime size pieces.
2 Tblsp butter

Put cloves, peppercorns, and bay leaf
   in cheesecloth bag.
Cook Tomatoes, undrained, cheesecloth bag,
   and a dash of salt on Top of Stove
   very slowly 30 minutes. Stir occasionally.
Add onion, sugar, bread, and butter.
Place in greased baking dish.

   When ready To bake, remove cheesecloth
      bag and contents and bake at 400°
      1 hour.

Serves 6

54

Potato Casserole

A delicious potato dish using <u>canned</u> potatoes!

2 cans small white potatoes
parsley, chopped
pepper
Dill seed
Oregano
1 can mushroom soup
1 soup can of milk
garlic powder
paprika

Drain potatoes and place in baking dish.
Sprinkle generously with parsley.
Season with pepper.
Sprinkle with a pinch of dill seed.
Sprinkle with 2 pinches oregano, crumbled.
Dilute 1 can mushroom soup with 1 can milk.
Stir 1/8 Tsp. garlic powder into soup.
Pour this over potatoes.
Sprinkle paprika over top.

When ready to bake, place baking dish
in 350° oven, covered, until hot —
about 45 minutes.

Serves 4-6

Fried Rice

This really special casserole can be made the main dish by adding shrimp, chicken, ham, or Turkey!

2 Tblsp. salad oil
1 bunch green onions, chopped. (Include some of the green Tops.)
1 cup diced celery - or more
2 cups cooked rice
    salt
2 Tblsp. soya sauce (or 3 if you like it strong.)
    Chopped, blanched almonds, browned in butter

Saute onions and celery in oil but do not brown
Add rice (I use precooked rice), salt, and soya sauce.
Mix and place in casserole.

When ready to bake, place in 350° oven for ½ hour - or less - until thoroughly heated.
Toss almonds on Top just before serving.

Serves 4

Noodles and Mushrooms

This is delicious with ham or any roast.

1 white onion
1 green pepper
½ cup salad oil
½ can cream style corn
1 can Tomato soup
1 box medium wide noodles
1 small can chopped or sliced ripe olives
1 small can mushrooms, drained
  grated cheese

Dice pepper and onions and fry slowly in
  oil until glossy.
Boil noodles 9 minutes.
Mix all ingredients together (except cheese)
  and place in casserole. Refrigerate.

When ready to bake, cover top with
  grated cheese. Place casserole in pan
  containing a small amount of warm
  water and bake at 350° for 1 hour.

If you wish to use it as a main dish,
  brown 1 pound of ground round or
  chuck and add to casserole.

Green Rice

Perfect for a luncheon with salad.

3 cups cooked white rice
2 1/2 cups milk
2 cups grated sharp cheese
2 eggs, beaten
2 Tsp. olive oil - or salad oil
1 cup chopped parsley
4 green onions, chopped fine
1 large Tsp. Worcestershire sauce

Mix all, season well with salt
and pepper, and place in
greased casserole.

When ready to bake, place in
350° oven for 45 minutes.

Serves 6

Gnocchi

This is a really impressive, fluffy and
   smooth side dish for any roast. IT
   can be served with gravy, or just
   butter.

2 cups milk, heated but <u>not boiling</u>
1/2 cup Cream of Wheat
1 Tsp. salt
1/4 cup margarine, chopped
   dash cayenne
1 cup cheddar cheese, grated
1 egg, beaten with a fork.

Place warm milk, Cream of Wheat, salt,
   margarine, and cayenne in double
   boiler and heat thoroughly until
   margarine is all melted. Stir often.
Remove from fire - add grated cheese.
Add the egg. (I add 1 Tblsp. of the warm
   mixture to the egg and stir lightly.
   Then another Tblsp. and stir. Do this 5
   Times, then add egg mixture to whole
   warm mixture. This way you will avoid
   danger of egg "stringing".)

Place in greased casserole and let stand
   at room temperature.

Bake at 350° for 1 hour until nice and
   brown on top.
If doubling (or more), decrease salt

Serves 4

Green and Yellow Rice

This is supposed to serve 8 but it won't because your guests will consume quantities!

3 cups boiled rice - use any kind - I use precooked.

¼ cup butter or margarine
4 beaten eggs
1 lb. grated sharp cheddar cheese - grate it at home - don't buy it already grated!
1 cup milks
1 pkg. frozen, chopped spinach - cooked and drained
1 Tblsp. chopped onion
1 Tblsp. Worcestershire Sauce
½ Teasp. each marjoram, thyme, rosemary, and salt.

Boil rice to obtain the 3 cups.
Melt butter and add to rice - unless you added it as with precooked rice.
Beat eggs and grate cheese.
Add milks to eggs - then add cheese - then spinach - and mix well, but gently. Add onion, Worcestershire, and seasonings. Set aside after placing in 2 qt casserole.
When ready, set casserole, uncovered, in pan of warm water and bake at 350° for 45 minutes. Serves 6?

60

Brown Rice Deluxe

And you'll like it! A West Coast recipe.

1 cup quick cooking brown rice
1 can (3½ oz.) french fried onions
2 cans Mushroom Soup
¼ cup stuffed green olives, sliced
1 can (2 oz.) mushroom stems and pieces
½ cup milk
¼ Teasp. pepper
¼ cup freshly grated Parmesan or
    cheddar cheese

Cook brown rice according to directions on box.
    Drain and place in 2 QT casserole
Add the onions, mushrooms, and olives - but
    save the juice from the mushrooms.
    Mix all gently.
In another bowl put the soup, milk,
    pepper, and juice from mushrooms.
    Set all aside.

When ready to bake, pour the mushroom
    soup mixture into rice mixture
    and mix all gently. Bake, uncovered,
    at 350° for 30 minutes. Then
    sprinkle cheese over the top. Bake
    for 10 more minutes.

Serves 6

Norfolk Noodles

Mighty Tasty!

12 oz. wide noodles
  1 cup fresh parsley, chopped
  1 pt. carton cottage cheese - large curd
  1 pt. carton commercial sour cream
  1 Tblsp. Worcestershire sauce
    dash Tobasco
  1 bunch green onions, chopped. Be sure
    to use some of the onion tops.
  1/2 cup grated sharp cheese
  1/2 Teasp. paprika

Boil noodles according to directions on
    the package. Drain.
While noodles are still hot, mix in all
    the remaining ingredients except
    cheese and paprika.
Place in a baking dish, preferably shallow.
Refrigerate.
When ready to bake, top with cheese
    and paprika. Place in 350° oven,
    uncovered, for 40 minutes or
    until hot through and cheese is
    melted.
  Serves 8

White Rice Browned

Our bachelor friend makes a whole meal
out of this!

½ cup butter or margarine
2 cups raw white rice
2¼ Tsp. salt
¼ Tsp. pepper
2 cans beef consomme
2 cups water
½ cup chopped, blanched almonds (I prepare
      these ahead - or buy them canned.)

Melt butter in large frying pan
Add rice
Cook over very slow fire, stirring often,
      until rice is golden brown.
Place in 2 QT. casserole.
Sprinkle on seasonings -

When ready to bake, add consomme,
      water, and nuts. Mix gently.
Cover and bake at 300° for 1 hour
      and 15 minutes. Do not stir.

Serves 10

Lazy Salad Sandwich

Try this for your next luncheon. It's fun to make - fun for your guests - and a real conversation piece!

Place about 3 lettuce leaves (preferably red lettuce if you can get it) on a dinner sized plate.

Put in the center a well-flavored egg sandwich (use chopped pickle, mayonnaise salt and pepper) and cut off the crusts but do not cut it in half. Also, boil an extra egg and save it, chopped, for later.

On the sandwich place 1 large or 2 smaller slices of peeled tomato.

On top of this put crab or shrimp.

Place a couple of olives and a pickled beet on the side.

Then have a huge bowl of really rich Thousand island type dressing. (To 1 cup of real mayonnaise I add 2 heaping Tblsp. chili sauce, 1 Tblsp. finely chopped green pepper, 1 Tblsp. chopped green onion and the chopped egg you saved.) Your guests cover their sandwich with the dressing.

You may serve potato chips if you like, but no bread is necessary. All is on one plate.

This may all be prepared in advance and assembled at the last minute.

Coronado Salad Ring

So delicious and complete that it needs
no dressing.

1 pkg. lime jello
1 pkg. lemon jello
2 cups hot water
10 oz. dry creamed cottage cheese (small curd)
1 #2 can crushed pineapple, well drained
2/3 cup chopped walnuts
1 cup pastry cream, not whipped
1 cup mayonnaise
1 Tblsp. horseradish (bottled type)

Dissolve the jellos in the hot water.
Add remaining ingredients in the
    order given.
Place in a wet ring mold and
    refrigerate until firm.
When ready to serve, unmold onto
    a platter. Fill center with fresh
    strawberries.

Serves 8

65

My Favorite French Dressing

2 cups olive or salad oil
1/2 cup red wine vinegar, garlic flavor
2 Tsp. salt
2 Tsp. freshly ground pepper
2 Tsp. wet mustard
2 Tsp. Worcestershire sauce

Beat with an egg beater and store in refrigerator in covered container. If it separates, just let it stand for a while at room Temperature.

Always shake well before using.

For Roquefort dressing, just add whatever amount of crumbled bleu cheese you like, and beat it along with rest of ingredients.

Add dressing to salad just before serving and Toss well.

Mixed Bean Salad

Ideal for a barbecue. A wonderfully
  "fool-proof" recipe!

1 can green beans - No. 303 size (2 cups)
1 can wax beans - Same size
1 can red kidney beans - Same size
1/2 cup chopped green pepper
3/4 cup sugar
2/3 cup cider vinegar
1/3 cup salad oil
1 Teasp. pepper
1 Teasp. salt

Drain canned beans well.
Add chopped green pepper To beans.
Combine remaining ingredients and
  mix well.
Now mix all Together and let stand,
  refrigerated, for 24 hours.
Drain off excess liquid before serving.

Serves 6 generously.

Parsley Dressing for Fresh Tomatoes

Entirely different - and can be made days ahead.

2 cups fresh parsley
½ cup chopped chives
1 cup sweet pickles, drained
2 cloves garlic
salt and pepper to suit

Cut the chives very fine (I use scissors)
Then put all the above ingredients through the food grinder twice. Use the small blade. Save any juice that may escape.
Then add:
    ½ cup olive oil
    ½ cup red wine vinegar
    ¼ cup Tarragon vinegar
    The juice from grinding
Mix all well and keep at room temperature for 24 hours in a covered jar. Then refrigerate.
Serve ice cold on platter of chilled, peeled, sliced Tomatoes.
Will keep, refrigerated, covered for 2 weeks.

Molded Salad

Perfect with clam dish on page 36.

1 pkg. lemon jello
1 1/2 Tblsp. vinegar
1/2 cup real mayonnaise
1/4 Tsp. salt
1/3 cup chopped celery
1 Tblsp. minced onion
1 cup chopped frozen spinach
 (Thawed and drained)
3/4 cup cottage cheese

Dissolve jello in 3/4 cup boiling water.
Add one cup cold water.
Add vinegar, mayonnaise, and salt.
Put in freezer Tray and chill until
 firm 1 inch around sides of Tray.
Turn into bowl and beat until fluffy.
Add celery, onion, spinach, and cottage
 cheese.

Place in 1 QT. mold and chill in
 refrigerator until firm.

Best done a day ahead.

Serves 6

Pineapple - Cheese Salad Ring

½ pound cottage cheese
1 cup whipped cream
1 Tblsp. gelatine
½ cup water
2½ cups grated pineapple, drained
2 Tblsp mayonnaise
½ Tsp. salt.

Rub cottage cheese through a
sieve. Add salt.
Soak gelatine in cold water and
dissolve over hot water.
Add cheese, mix well.
Add mayonnaise, pineapple, and cream.
Chill in ring until firm.

When ready, unmold and serve with
a dressing of mayonnaise plus a
little lemon juice and a little
whipped cream. Use fresh fruit in
center of ring.

70

Spinach Salad

Different!. And so healthy!.

2 cellophane pkgs. fresh spinach
Salad oil
lemon juice

Wash spinach - shake gently To dry - cut
off all stems.
Then, using scissors, cut spinach leaves in
one inch wide pieces.
Sprinkle a little oil on leaves - Then a
little lemon juice. Barely dampen The
leaves - do not saturate!.
Refrigerate.

Serve with a side dish of:

Chili Dressing

1 cup mayonnaise
1/4 cup chili sauce
juice of 1 lemon
minced green onion To Taste

Mix well and chill until ready To serve.

Serves 6 To 8

71

Vermicelli Salad
Really ideal for The hot summertime

1 12 oz. pkg. vermicelli
5 hard boiled eggs, chopped
5 stalks of celery, chopped
6 good-sized sweet pickles, chopped
¼ small yellow onion, chopped fine
     salt To Taste
1½ cups real mayonnaise
2 cans shrimp or crab (4½ oz. size)
        drained, washed gently, and chilled
   Paprika

Break vermicelli in half and boil as
    directed on The package. Drain
    Thoroughly in colander and run
    under cold water well To prevent
    sticking.
When vermicelli is cool, add next 6
    ingredients and mix well. Refrigerate
Just before serving, add shrimp or
    crab and Toss lightly.
Sprinkle with paprika and serve To
    10 or 12 happy guests!

Dressing for Coleslaw

1/3 cup real mayonnaise
3 Tblsp. milk
1 or 2 Tblsp. pickle juice - depending
   on how tart you like it. (Use
   juice from sweet pickles, not dill.)
Minced green onion or green onion Tops

Mix mayonnaise and milk
Stir in pickle juice.
Add onions.
Chill.

When ready To serve, add To 1
   pkg. fresh coleslaw or amount
   To serve 4. Toss well.

Potato Salad

4 cups diced, boiled potatoes
1 cup diced cucumber
3 Tblsp. minced onion
1½ Tsp. salt
½ Tsp. pepper
3 hard boiled eggs, diced

Mix the above and toss with the
following dressing:

Dressing

1½ cups sour cream (commercial)
½ cup mayonnaise
¼ cup vinegar
¾ Tsp. celery seed
1 Tsp. wet mustard

Chill salad until ready to serve.

Serves 6 amply

Lewiston Salad Dressing

My mother's favorite! Good on any kind of salad.

Juice of one large lemon, strained
6 Tblsp. olive oil (no substitute)
1 Teasp. salt
½ Teasp. pepper
½ clove garlic - if desired

Mix in the order given and stir well.
Make it several hours ahead of time
    and let stand at room temperature.
When ready to serve, remove the
    garlic and again stir the
    dressing well.

For a salad serving 4 persons.

Cream Dressing for Salads

1 pt. real mayonnaise
2 Tblsp. (generous) anchovy paste
3 Tblsp. Tarragon or red wine vinegar
1 Tblsp. scraped onion
1 small clove garlic, minced
6 fillet of anchovy, chopped
    (if you omit This, double The paste.)
1 Tblsp. chopped parsley
1 Tblsp. chives or green onion Tops, cut
    fine

Mix vinegar with mayonnaise
Add other ingredients. Mix well.
Chill.

I serve This on a salad of only
    romaine lettuce.

If you yearn for a roquefort cream
dressing, just grate desired amount
of bleu cheese into dressing and mix
well. Omit all anchovy.

Can easily be made a day or so ahead.

Be sure to add all salad dressings
just before serving - and Toss well.

Cranberry Salad Mold

2 cans jellied cranberry sauce
2 envelopes gelatine
1/2 cup cold water
1/2 Tsp. salt
2/3 cup chopped walnuts
2/3 cup diced apples
1/2 cup chopped celery

Crush sauce with a fork.
Put gelatine in water - let stand 2 minutes. (Do This in a small, flat bowl.) Place dish in pan of boiling water after gelatine is absorbed! Let stand until dissolved. Stir a bit.
Add gelatine to cranberry sauce and stir until smooth. Place in refrigerator for 1 or 2 hours until partially jelled.
Add remaining ingredients and pour into mold. Chill until firm.

Unmold when ready and pass mayonnaise when serving. Add a little red wine vinegar to mayonnaise if you want it more tart.
If made a day ahead, keep in refrigerator covered with aluminum foil.

Pear Ring Mold

1 pkg. lime jello
canned pear halves
2 pkgs. cream cheese

Make lime jello according to directions on pkg.
Take half of it and pour over some canned
pears in quart ring mold. Place in refrigerator to "set" a little. (1 or 2 hours)
Take other half of jello and add the cream
cheese which has been put through a sieve.
Let this stand at room temperature until
the first mixture has "set" partially.
Then pour jello-cheese mixture over jello-
pear mixture and return mold to
refrigerator to completely jell.

This can be served with 2 or 3 cups fresh
grapes in center. Mix grapes into following sauce:

2 egg yolks well beaten
1 Tblsp sugar
a little salt
2 Tblsp. Tarragon vinegar
Cook above in double boiler very carefully until pretty thick. Chill, and
when cold, add ½ pt. or less of
whipped cream. Add grapes.

For the whole mold serve a dressing of
mayonnaise with a little salad oil
and lemon juice to taste added.

78

Whiskey Ice Box Cake

A delectable dessert for 12.

2 envelopes gelatine
1/2 cup cold water
1/2 cup boiling water
6 eggs, separated
7 or 8 Tblsp. whiskey
1 cup sugar
1 Teasp. lemon juice
1 pt. whipping cream
3 pkgs. lady fingers, split

Soak gelatine in cold water. Then add
   boiling water and dissolve.
Beat egg yolks until thick.
Add whiskey very slowly.
Beat in the sugar.
Add lemon juice
Stir in gelatine and chill a short time.
Whip cream and fold it in.
Beat egg whites and fold in.
Line sides and bottom of a spring form
   pan (about 12") with split lady fingers.
Pour the mixture in slowly. When about
   half way, put in layer of lady fingers.
Then, when filled, place a layer of lady fingers
   on top in a design.
Chill overnight in the refrigerator.

Washington Cookies

Our favorites!

1½ cups flour
1 Teasp. soda
1 Teasp. salt
1 cup margarine
3/4 cup brown sugar
3/4 cup granulated sugar

2 eggs
1 Teasp. vanilla
1 cup chopped walnuts
2 cups rolled oats
1 pkg. chocolate bits

Sift flour, measure, and sift again with soda and salt.

Cream margarine with both sugars.

Beat eggs into margarine-sugar mixture.
Add vanilla and mix well.

Stir in dry ingredients.
Add nuts, oats, and bits and mix all thoroughly.

Drop on greased cookie sheet (about 1 Tblsp. batter for each cookie) and bake 12-15 minutes at 350° until light brown.

Makes about 6 dozen delicious cookies

Butterscotch Toffee Heavenly Delight

As good as it sounds!

1½ cups whipping cream
1 can (5½ oz.) butterscotch syrup (Topping)
½ Teasp. vanilla extract
1 unfrosted angel cake (9½")
¾ lb. English Toffee, crushed (put through food grinder using largest blade.)

Whip cream until it starts to Thicken.
Add butterscotch syrup and vanilla slowly and continue beating until Thick.
Cut cake into 3 layers- horizontally.
Spread The butterscotch mixture on the layers and sprinkle each generously with crushed Toffee.
Put cake back Together again and frost The Top and sides with butterscotch mixture and sprinkle Them, Too, with Toffee.
Place cake in The refrigerator and chill for a minimum of 6 hours.

Serves 12

Annapolis Angel Food Dessert

Hard on your dieting guests, but
  They'll never resist it!

2 bags chocolate bits
6 Teasp. warm water
3 eggs, separated
3 Tblsp. powdered sugar
1/2 cup chopped walnuts
1 1/2 cups whipping cream
1 unfrosted angel cake (9 1/2")

Melt chocolate bits in Top of double boiler.
Add water and stir to mix. When all is
  melted and mixed, remove from fire.
Beat egg yolks with powdered sugar and
  add to chocolate mixture slowly.
Add chopped nuts. (Don't give up! This
  is usually hard to mix!)
Beat egg whites until stiff and fold into
  above mixture.
Whip cream and fold it in.
Place frosting in refrigerator for 12 hours.
Cut angel cake horizontally into 3 layers.
  Cover each layer with frosting - reassemble
  cake - frost top and sides and place in
  refrigerator for another 12 hours.
Serves 12   82

Bremerton Bourbon Balls

No-cook cookies!.

2½ cups crushed vanilla wafers
   (Most of a 12 oz. pkg.)
2 Tblsp. cocoa
1 cup confectioners sugar (sift before
   measuring.)
1 cup chopped walnuts
3 Tblsp corn syrup or honey
¼ cup bourbon or brandy or rum
   confectioners sugar for topping

Mix well the crumbs, cocoa, the
   1 cup sugar, and the nuts.
Add the corn syrup and liquor. Mix
   all very thoroughly.
Form into one inch balls, then roll
   in confectioners sugar. That's
   all!

Note: Keep in a covered tin. These
   are even better the second day.

Makes 3 to 3½ dozen cookies.

Cracker Pie

Be sure **To** make This!

3 egg whites
1 cup sugar
1 Teasp. baking powder
1/2 Teasp. vanilla
3/4 cup chopped nuts (walnuts or pecans)
1 cup cracker crumbs (RITZ CRACKERS or
        WAVERLY WAFERS)
    Ice cream (vanilla)

Beat egg whites until stiff.
Add sugar, baking powder, and vanilla.
    Mix each in well.
Fold in nuts.
Add cracker crumbs (crumbs are easily
        obtained by using a rolling pin.)
Mix all carefully and pour into
        well greased 8" pie plate.
Bake 30 minutes at 350°. Let cool in
    its plate but outside oven.
Cut in wedges, Top with ice cream,
        and serve To 6 happy
            dessert lovers!
Pie freezes well, Too.

84

Creme Chocolate

Fun To serve in after dinner coffee cups!

1 pkg. chocolate bits
4 Tblsp. cold water
5 eggs, separated
   whipped cream

Put chocolate bits in pan with the
   cold water. Stir over low heat, with
   wooden spoon, until well blended.

Remove from the fire and slowly stir
   in the 5 egg yolks which have
   been well beaten. Mix well.

Fold in the 5 stiffly beaten whites.
   Continue until all is well blended.

Pour into after dinner coffee cups and
   store in refrigerator at least 5
   hours - preferably overnight.

Serve in cups with a bit of whipped
   cream - unsweetened, as this is a
   very rich dessert.

Fills 10 cups.

85

Pasadena Peach Delight

The perfect dessert for a hot summer
evening! And particularly good after seafood.

1 pkg. ladyfingers (about 10)
   Peach Brandy
2 pkgs. frozen sliced peaches (semi-thawed)
½ pint whipping cream
1 teasp. sugar
4 or 5 drops vanilla or almond extract

Line bottom and sides of ice cube tray
   with split ladyfingers.
Moisten ladyfingers with brandy but
   do not saturate.
Arrange partly thawed peach slices over
   ladyfingers.
Whip cream, adding sugar and flavoring.
Top the dessert with whipped cream.
If you wish to be extra fancy, sprinkle
   top of whipped cream with toasted
   slivered almonds.
Cover ice tray with wax paper and
   freeze for at least 6 hours.
When serving, cut across tray to form
   narrow slices. (Remove from freezer
   20 minutes before serving.)
Serves 8

Chocolate-Mint Angel Cake

Delicious, pretty to see, and made a
day ahead!

1 Angel cake (about 10" size)
1 Qt. whipping cream
1 cup granulated sugar
4 heaping Tblsp. cocoa
    dash of salt
1 Tsp. Peppermint Extract
    Bitter chocolate

When cake is cool, slice crosswise
    in 4 layers. Set aside while
    you make the following filling.

Mix together the cream, sugar, cocoa,
    salt, and Extract. Put in
    refrigerator for 1 hour. Then
    whip to proper consistency for
    icing.

Now put the cake back together
    again, icing each layer as you
    go. Ice sides. Grate bitter
    chocolate on the top of iced
    cake. You may add some slivered
    almonds (which you have browned
    in butter) for decoration.
Make the day before and refrigerate
    overnight.

Serves 10 generously and 12 easily.

87

Lemon Ice Cream

So light, delicate, and refreshing!

1 cup granulated sugar
7 Tblsp. fresh lemon juice (about 4 lemons)
2 cups Half and Half (found at your grocer's
    milk counter)

Mix together the sugar and lemon juice.
Stir it carefully into the Half and Half.
Pour into freezer tray in top of your
    refrigerator.
Stir gently while it is freezing. I do this
    after 40 minutes and after 40 minutes
    more, using a fork to crush any lumps.
Finish freezing. Remove from freezer about
    10 minutes before serving—less in hot
    climate.

                Serves 5

Orange Ice Cream

Easy—and with a different flavor!

2 pints vanilla ice cream—softened, not melted.
2 small cans frozen orange juice, undiluted
2 generous ounces Grand Marnier liqueur

Soften ice cream and thaw orange juice.
Mix all together well and put in freezer tray.
Freeze it—Tho' it won't get really hard.
Serve in sherbets with a cookie or slice
    of cake.

              Serves 8

Christmas Cookies

An annual affair at our house. Really glamorous cookies!

6 cups sifted flour
1 Teasp. salt
2 cups butter (1 lb.) no substitute!
2 cups granulated sugar
4 unbeaten eggs
2 Teasp. vanilla extract

Sift flour and salt together.

Cream butter until soft. Gradually add sugar, creaming after each addition until it is light and fluffy.

Add eggs and vanilla to butter-sugar mixture and mix well. (May become lumpy but keep mixing until lumps are small.)

Add flour-salt mixture a little at a time and mix well.

Cover bowl and refrigerate at least 5 hours.

Roll out dough to 1/8 inch thickness. Use a small portion of dough at a time and be sure to flour your board, rolling pin, and cutters often or dough will stick to board.

Cut out shapes with cookie cutters, dipping them in flour each time.

((Cont'd))

89

Christmas Cookies (cont'd)

Place on ungreased cookie sheet and bake at 375° for about 10 minutes or until light brown around the edges.

When cool, frost as described below.

We use as cutters a star, a bell, a tree, and a gingerbread boy who makes a fine Santa.

Makes 70 to 90 cookies depending on which cutters you choose.

Frosting for Christmas Cookies

4 egg whites
½ teasp. Cream of Tartar
½ teasp. vanilla
5 cups sifted confectioners sugar
candy cake decorations and food coloring

Now comes the fun!

Beat egg whites with Cream of Tartar and vanilla until foamy.
Gradually beat in the sifted powdered sugar until frosting stands in firm peaks.
Now gather the family around the table.
Divide the frosting among 5 custard or teacups. Tint 4 of the cups with food coloring — red, blue, green, and yellow. If necessary use more than 1 bottle of coloring each because you want bright colors! The 5th cup will be white.

90

Frosting for Christmas Cookies (Cont'd)

Place an individual butter spreader or small
  knife in each cup.
Have several bottles of cake decorations nearby.

Now you are ready! Give each cookie a
  complete "color job". Green Christmas
  Trees then have garlands of all colors—
  and ornaments of cake decorations. Each
  star is gaily colored - perhaps striped -
  and maybe has multi-colored tips. Dots
  and designs of all kinds grace your bells.
  Santa is complete with white beard and
  belt, blue eyes, and buttons down the front.
  My husband delights our children with
  his gingerbread boy transformed into
  a sailor in blues proudly wearing his
  campaign ribbons!

These are really gay. Just be sure you
  give each cookie a complete coating.
  None of the cookie itself should show -
    just the decorative frosting. Have
    fun - and let your imagination have
    a field day!

(If frosting hardens, add a few drops of
  hot water.)

Quick but Tasty Desserts with no Advance Preparation

It's easy to keep the ingredients for several of these on hand ready for unexpected guests.

① Top a chilled slice of pineapple with a scoop of pineapple ice. Make a slight indentation on top of ice and pour in 2 or 3 Tblsp. Creme de Menthe.

② Top coffee ice cream with grated semi-sweet chocolate.

③ Top a serving of vanilla ice cream with several Tblsp. of Cointreau.

④ Top mocha ice cream with hot chocolate sauce.

⑤ Top lime ice with crushed chocolate bits.

⑥ Top a saucer of fresh raspberries with several Tblsp. commercial sour cream. Top sour cream with one half Tblsp. brown sugar.

My Favorite Dip

2 pkgs. cream cheese
2 beef bouillon cubes
   boiling water
   mayonnaise
5 green onions, minced
1/8 Tsp. Spice Islands Beau Monde
   Seasoning

Cream Together the cheese.
Dissolve bouillon cubes in smallest
   possible amount of water (about
   1/4 cup.) Add To cheese.
Add onion and Beau Monde.
Mix well and refrigerate.

When ready To serve, add mayonnaise and mix until dip is
   right consistency.

Cheese Roll

You'll love it!

1 lb. yellow cheese
2 pkg. cream cheese (3 oz. each)
1 cup cashew nuts
2 cloves garlic, minced
  paprika

Put yellow cheese through food grinder,
  using the finest blade.
Soften and whip the cream cheese.
Put cashews through grinder - same blade.
Mix all ingredients, except paprika, well.
Shape into a roll about 1 1/2 inches in
  diameter.
Then roll in lots of paprika. The roll
  should be really red on the outside
Wrap in wax paper and refrigerate.
When ready to serve, slice very thin
  and place on round crackers.
This keeps well in your refrigerator
  or may be frozen.

94

Caviar Dip

1 8 oz. pkg cream cheese
1 pint commercial sour cream
1 Tblsp. minced yellow onion
1 small jar black or red caviar.

Whip cheese and mix with sour
    cream.

Add onion.

Add caviar and mix all well.

Refrigerate.

Serve with waffle style chips
    To 12-14 guests.

Clam Canapes

One of my most used recipes.

1 pkg. cream cheese
1 can minced clams, drained
   salt to taste
   dash of red pepper
3/4 Teasp. Worcestershire Sauce
1 Teasp. minced green onion

Whip the cheese with a fork.
Add the clams and mix well.
Add remaining ingredients and
   whip well.
Place in the refrigerator in a
   covered dish.

When ready to serve, heap generously
   on plain white salty crackers and
   bake at 300° for 20 minutes.
You may sprinkle with paprika
   for "looks."

Double Cheese Dip

1 Triangle Roquefort cheese – or about
   1/3 cup Bleu cheese
2 pkgs. cream cheese (3 oz. size)
1 Tblsp. chopped fresh parsley
2 Tblsp. chopped green onions
   dash of cayenne
   dash of Worcestershire sauce
2 heaping Tblsp. mayonnaise
4 level Tblsp. commercial sour cream
1/4 Teasp. horseradish
   salt to taste

Cream cheeses together.
Add remaining ingredients – mix well –
   do not refrigerate, just set aside.
When ready, serve with potato chips.

If you place this in the refrigerator
   for several hours, it will harden and
   become an excellent dip for carrot
   sticks.

97

Filled French Rolls

Fun To make - and fun To eat!

8 French rolls
½ cup softened margarine - not melted
½ cup grated Parmesan cheese
2 Tblsp. salad oil
½ cup finely chopped fresh parsley
1 clove garlic, finely chopped
½ Teasp. sweet basil
    salt To Taste

Turn each roll on its side and cut into
    ½ inch slices - but do not cut all The
    way Through The roll.
Make The filling by blending The margarine
    with The remaining ingredients.
Spread The filling between each slice.
Wrap each roll individually in aluminum
    foil. Set aside until needed.

Bake in a 375° oven for 20 minutes.
Serve in The foil. Each person Keeps his
    roll hot by rewrapping in The foil.
    Wonderful for a barbecue in your
    patio!
Rolls may be frozen in Their foil wrappers.
    If not Thawed, bake 10 minutes longer.

Cold Sauce for Ham

2 cucumbers - peel and remove seeds
1 cup real mayonnaise.
5 Teasp. prepared horseradish
4 Teasp. wet mustard
1 Teasp. salt
   dash of red pepper

Chop cucumbers. There should be about
   1²/3 cups.
Mix well with remaining ingredients.
Serve chilled.

Hot Sauce for Ham

1 glass currant or boysenberry jelly.
   rind (grated) and juice of 1 orange
¼ Teasp. nutmeg
¼ Teasp. cinnamon
⅛ Teasp. powdered ginger
1 jigger port wine

Combine all except port.

When ready, place in Top of double
   boiler until hot.
Add port just before you take it
   off the heat. Stir all gently.

San Francisco Cocktail

Before a festive luncheon it is often fun to serve an unusual cocktail. Try this!

2 Fifths of White Port
8 oz. light Rum
  juice of 4 lemons
  Maraschino cherries - or fresh strawberries

Chill the Port
Add the Rum and lemon juice
Mix well, place in a glass container
  and refrigerate.

When ready to serve, place a cherry
  or fresh strawberry in each glass,
  stir the cocktail well, and serve
  very cold in wine or martini
  glasses. You may add a little
  ice to the shaker to keep it
  cold.

Serves 12 - 16

Ideas

Surround your Christmas Turkey with This:
   Place canned peach halves in baking dish.
   Fill centers with mincemeat.
   Cover bottom of dish with peach juice.
   Place in 300° oven until hot.

Green Beans

   Boil 2 pkgs. green beans 7 minutes.
      Drain and place in 1½ qt. casserole.
   Mix 1 can undiluted mushroom soup
      with ¼ soup can milk. Pour over beans.
   Just before baking, fold in 1 can French
      fried onions, saving some for top.
   Bake, uncovered, at 300° for 35 minutes.

Green Salad

   Crumble 1 wedge (1¼ oz.) roquefort cheese
      into 1 small carton sour cream.
   Mash cheese and stir until fairly smooth.
   Add 1 heaping Tblsp. mayonnaise, juice of
      ½ a lemon, 1 green onion (minced), and
      at least ⅛ teasp. black pepper-freshly
      ground if possible.
   Refrigerate, covered.
   Just before adding dressing to salad,
      add 2 small cans chilled, drained,
      seedless grapes to salad greens.
   Toss all and serve.

Index

Main Dishes

With Chicken

With Beef

103

Main Dishes

With Beef (cont'd.)

Wild Rice Party Casserole	17
Meat Balls	25
Picnic Barbecue	31
Pizza Pie	35
Sophisticated Stew	42
Spaghetti Sauce	50
Stroganoff Bake (veal)	8
Sausage and Veal	20
Veal Vermouth	38

With Lamb

Lamb Shanks Deluxe	28

With Pork

Cambridge Chicken with Ham	6
Savory Sausage Casserole	9
Sausage Casserole for Six	15
Sausage and Veal	20
Sausages and Apples	23
Not Navy Beans	40

Main Dishes

With Seafood

105

Main Dishes

With Beans

Spanish Bean Pot — 11

Not Navy Beans — 40

With Eggs

Egg-Asparagus-Mushroom Casserole — 19

Rice and Deviled Eggs with Tuna — 47

Side Dishes

With Rice

Mushrooms and Rice — 52

Fried Rice — 56

Green Rice — 58

Green and Yellow Rice — 60

Brown Rice Deluxe — 61

White Rice Browned — 63

With Potatoes

Potato Casserole — 55

Side Dishes

With Macaroni or Noodles

Miscellaneous

Salads

Odds and Ends (Cont'd)

Note

One half the author's profit from this book is given to

The National Cystic Fibrosis Research Foundation
521 Fifth Avenue
New York 17, N.Y.

Notes

Notes

Notes

Notes

Notes

Notes

Notes

Notes

Notes

Notes